Blessed Art Thou

Images of the Virgin Mary in the Ahmanson Collection

Blessed Art Thou
Images of the Virgin Mary in the Ahmanson Collection

Ahmanson Gallery, 2019
Irvine, California

PINATUBO PRESS

Contents

Introduction

One of the surprising and fun things about working with John Silvis and Ann Hirou to create our semi-annual art shows is that I learn things about our collection I didn't realize. The first one was the sculpture show *Define Gravity.* John came to me and suggested a sculpture show. I said I didn't collect sculpture. He said, Well, you have this and this and this ... Bemused, I had to admit, Yes, I collect sculpture.

Well, the same thing happened earlier this year when Ann Hirou suggested we do a Mary show, a Mother and Child show. What? I thought. We don't have enough images to do a whole show. And ... you guessed it. She started listing them.

So, for once we are going to have a show that fits the liturgical season. Opening a few weeks before Advent in the Christian calendar, this show will focus often on the Virgin Mary and Christ.

Images begin with the Annunciation in a painting called *Overshadowed* by Patty Wickman. There Mary is today's girl next door at home in a very present bedroom. A German wood relief from around 1500 tells the same story in a very different way.

The Nativity, in numerous versions, is next. Linda Syddick Napaltjarri sets the coming of Christ in a traditional Australian Aboriginal land painting. For William Kurelek, Christ is born in Canada, in many places in Canada in fact. Then, in a climate more like the one in which Christ actually lived, Alfonso Castillo Orta brings Christ into the world in a Mexican sheepherding hill town.

Next we see pictures of Mary adoring her baby son. Two from Middle and Northern Europe around 1500 show Mary nursing him. Henry Moore sculpted Christ on his mother's lap. Barbara Hepworth gives us a Christ held by his mother in black and white, a memorial to her own son who died in a tragic plane accident. Jacob Epstein shows a slightly older Jesus. Mary Cassatt's pastel sketch *A Kiss for Baby Anne (#1)* may not be intended to be Mary and Jesus, but it is unmistakably in the deep tradition of the unique relationship of Mother and Child.

Georges Rouault shows us Mary at the Crucifixion. Others take us to the moments just after his death when Mary cradles her dead son's body in her arms, one of them by Sun Xun paints Michelangelo's *Pietà* on the pages of an old German Bible.

Overleaf: Alfonso Castillo Orta, *Tree of Life Nativity,* Detail, 2014
Opposite: Patrociño Barela, *The Virgin of Guadalupe,* Detail, 1940

9

But that isn't the end of the story. With Edward Burra we rise to heaven for the moment when Christ crowns his mother Queen of Heaven. Patrociño Barela and Marie Romero Cash give two very different portrayals of the Virgin of Guadalupe, the miraculous appearance of Mary to a Mexican peasant.

And there are more. What perhaps surprises me even more than the fact that we do collect images of the Virgin and Child is how varied those images are. This is a deep human relationship, one we all experience from one side or the other or both. It is ineffable and yet part of everyone's existence.

Of course, we now face the reality that a child may not come into the world through the body of the woman whose DNA that child will bear. DNA is bought and sold, commodified. We have no idea where that reality will lead.

But, if these images show us anything, they are filled with the scent of sacredness. There is something there. Mother and Child. Often fraught. Sometimes destructive. Other times, more times, we hope, nurturing, loving. It is a relationship at the heart of our humanness. What better season to ponder its meaning than Advent.

We welcome you to *Blessed Art Thou* and hope the show both refreshes you and gives you food for thought.

Roberta Green Ahmanson
Edinburgh
17 August 2019

Opposite: Mary Cassatt, *A Kiss for Baby Anne (#1)*, Detail, 1897

Gate of Heaven

During a recent trip to Venice and Milan I had the opportunity to visit lavishly adorned historic chapels, cathedrals, and monasteries. With the images from the most recent exhibition in the Ahmanson gallery, *Blessed Art Thou: Images of the Virgin Mary in the Ahmanson Collection,* in my mind, it was especially meaningful to experience sculptures and paintings of Mary in diverse contexts, and it illuminated both the prevalence and weight of her character in Western art history. One of the earliest images of Mary has been attributed to an ancient baptistry painting in Deir ez-Zor, Syria, and many examples can be found throughout Europe in the early days of the Orthodox church. In later centuries the Madonna became the most recognizable depiction of the Christian faith, with the Madonna and Child being the most frequently painted subject matter. This motif is so powerful because it simultaneously represents a universal image of motherly love and the core doctrines of the Christian faith: the Incarnation and the Virgin Birth.

Blessed Art Thou: Images of the Virgin Mary in the Ahmanson Collection, features singular works by nineteen artists that engage with the subject of the Virgin Mary and Christ. The selection of artwork spans five centuries, and includes paintings, drawings, and sculptures; the devotional sensibility of each image articulates the deep, personal journey of faith that the Ahmansons have embarked on as a couple. One prominent work in particular, *The Virgin of Guadalupe,* by Mexican American artist Patrociño Barela, is especially profound. Barela was a self-taught artist and an important figure in twentieth-century Hispanic and New Mexican art. He used a unique approach to carve sculptures of Mary, Jesus, and the Saints, making each from a single piece of wood. His personal commitment to the visual exploration of Christian theology is embodied in the preciousness of his technique and his understanding of God among us.

Bookended by images of the *Madonna and Child,* with the oldest work being an oil painting by an unknown Flemish painter from the early 1500s, and the most recent one being a contemporary, assemblage sculpture by Canadian artist Ale Groen from 2018, each art work reveals glimpses of theological concepts of their respective eras. The placement of the works in the exhibition is organized around the most commonly depicted themes of Mary throughout art history: the Annunciation, Nativity, Madonna and Child, Pietà, and Mary, Mother of God. Other topics that have been interesting to artists and their patrons are the Assumption, the Mother of God, and the Sorrows of Mary, all of which are seminal representations of the Christian life of faith.

A recent painting by Patty Wickman, titled *Overshadowed* (2001), is a captivating, contemporary interpretation of the Annunciation. Similar to other historic paintings on this theme, the presence of the Holy Spirit is represented by a bright ray of light; in Wickman's painting she chooses a common bedside lamp to visualize the presence of the Holy Spirit. The young girl's hands are positioned so they create a shadow in an image of a dove. She is kneeling on the ground in surrender to the angel Gabriel, and yet the chaos of the messy bedroom and the apprehensive look on her face give the viewer a sense that her life is about to transform dramatically. One can imagine that this is how a young Mary felt in light of the overwhelming gift of being chosen as the Mother of God.

The softness of the pastel drawing by Mary Cassatt, *A Kiss for Baby Anne #1* (1897), captures the special bond between a mother and child. While it may not directly reference the traditional religious image of Mary and Jesus, it nonetheless hints at the sacredness of the tender touch of a mother. In art history Mary is increasingly seen as a link to human nature and earthly experience, which speaks to a larger desire for human dignity. Engaged in the quintessentially female endeavors of being a mother and a nurturer, the icon of Mary provides many cultures with an archetype of womanhood.

Contemporary scholars are acknowledging the importance of Mary as an inclusive symbol of the feminine in Western history. Likewise, Protestant theologians are reassessing the importance of women in the Bible, and in particular Mary, for is there anyone better to emulate than Mary, Mother of God? Contemporary culture presents many versions of what it means to be a woman, and in some ways it is elevating the uniqueness of motherhood. As we collectively examine different facets of her role both in Christianity and art history, her timeless qualities remain true: faithfulness, devotion, humility, purity. The contemplative depth of the art works in *Blessed Art Thou* portrays the ways in which Mary has captured the hearts and minds of artists throughout several centuries and created powerful images of transcendence.

John Silvis
Curator

Blessed Art Thou

Under Your Protection

An avant-garde poet exchanges meditation techniques with a white-robed Norbertine monk; an evangelical college professor learns about the next Burning Man from a downtown L.A. gallerist; the poet laureate of California gets a field report from a Baptist youth pastor; a Hindu and a Hesychast discuss the flavor profile of the cheese table—no one who has been to a gathering that celebrates the opening of an Ahmanson exhibition will ever have felt it to be just another Los Angeles social event. In fact, surveying the bewildering multiverse of Southern California society, it would be hard to imagine a gathering that more successfully brings regularly segregated groups together. Which is to say, in fissiparous America, the crowd assembled on the occasion an Ahmanson show itself constitutes an accomplishment.

But there is something about the *Blessed Art Thou* exhibition that represents the character of the Ahmanson collection and its disparate admirers especially well. Mary, it could be argued, is the heart of this collection (indeed—there were so many images of Mary that not even all of them are represented here). She foregrounds the collection's theological flavoring without overpowering the visual palette. Mary offers a bridge between the explicitly religious and secular works within the collection, and between the explicitly religious and less explicitly religious viewers who enjoy the festive Ahmanson celebrations. After all, Mary the Jewish mother is revered by Muslims, has earned the grudging respect of many a secularist, and for Christians of all stripes she, of course, remains *Theotokos,* the Mother of God. The Virgin provides aesthetic shelter to this unexpected range of friends just as she covered the faithful with her mantle in the *Madonna della Misericordia* icons of ages past.

But to appeal, however playfully, to Mary's protection (*sub tuum praesidium,* "under your protection," is our earliest recorded prayer to her[1]) is an ironically dangerous thing to do. It means we might not be safe among these images, if by safety we mean preserving the brittle encasements of our egos. To appeal to Mary in this way means this is not a show meant to tickle the senses. Nor is it a series of images that function as a score card in the ongoing Protestant/Catholic debate about the whether or not Mary had original sin or children after Jesus. Still less is it merely an attempt to convince the secular art world of the visual

---

[1] Maxwell Johnson, *"Sub tuum Praesidium:* The *Theotokos* in Christian Life and Worship before Ephesus," *Pro Ecclesia 17,* no. 1 (Winter 2008): 52-75.

Left: Georges Rouault, *Christ en Croix,* Detail, 1930

The first is the mess of a wood-carved Hungarian church interior at the dawn of the Reformation, a crowded room of rumpled folds. Master Paul of Leutschau (or Levoča) gives us a Mary who seems a bit annoyed to be distracted from her reading. With an inquiring, no-nonsense stare, she—well acquainted with biological facts—interrogates the angel, "How can this be, since I am still a Virgin?" (Luke 1:34). The answer is in the window. It is, after all, the Holy Spirit, not an intermediary, who will overshadow her (Luke 1:35).[11] Satisfied, she offers her consent—and consent is the watchword without which no modern Mariology can survive. Paul's Mary is not to be trifled with, but is also prepared to offer her cooperation in procuring the salvation of the world.

And then there are our own modern messes, especially those of teenage girls. In her 2001 painting, Patty Wickman has accomplished what Henry Ossawa Tanner managed a century before—that is, to make the Annunciation convincing all over again. Here too Mary is over-shadowed, the dove being a shadow puppet created by her hands and cast on her breast thanks to a bedroom lamp. This gesture also conveys that the event is impossible without Mary's full consent. On the right Wickman has summarized traditional Mariology. The empty closet and cage signify her emptiness—this is a virginal birth. The padlock evokes the *hortus conclusus* (enclosed garden), one of Mary's great medieval titles (Song of Solomon 4:12). The telephone evokes her constant prayer. Even the childhood photo seems to suggest the great legends of Mary's cloistered youth that come down to us through the early apocryphal text, the *Protoevangelium of James*.

But on the left hand side of the canvas, everything changes. This is a Mary who forgot to clean her room. The unmade bed and half-open drawers evoke her normality and ours. It is as if Wickman is suggesting God meets us in our everyday lives or not at all. The strewn stuffed animals of this regular teenager reveal she is not quite prepared to leave childhood behind. On this side of the canvas the artist places the shade that blocks the light. But even if this suggests sin, it was a shade that was gracefully removed. The empty chair might be a nod to the oft-forgotten revolutionary Mary, who prophecies that "he will cast down the mighty from their seat" (Luke 1:52). But most importantly perhaps, Wickman's Mary manages to be sexual without being sexualized, something that is nearly impossible to accomplish in our advertising-saturated age.

Nativity

The nativity scene—having long reached the iconographical saturation point—constitutes the most risk for any collector. Cliché seems inevitable. But the images in this collection avoid it by hurling us into the present through the ministrations of the Canadian painter William Kurelek. A look at Kurelek's 1957 self-portrait—flanked by Our Lady of Perpetual Help and the shrine to Mary at Lourdes—conveys that when it comes to the Virgin Mary, he is as tra-ditional as it gets. Still, just as Rogier van der Weyden placed his fifteenth-century patrons in Bethlehem, Kurelek, animated by the same piety, does the same for modern Canadians.

[11] Luke employs the same Greek term used to describe the *Shekinah* glory hovering over the temple. Darrell Bock, *Luke 1:1-9:50* (Baker, 1994), 122.

Opposite: Master Paul of Leutschau (Levoča), *Annunciation,* Detail, circa 1500

His 1975 *Stand in for the Christmas Stable* is the answer to Edward Hopper's famous painting, *Gas* (1940), fulfilling the latter's latent spiritual potential. Commenting on this painting, Kurelek writes that he rejoiced, "I'd never thought of a garage as being a beautiful building." [12]

In the same way, what is missing in the gritty street scenes painted and etched in the early twentieth-century by the Ashcan school is delivered by Kurelek, who re-envisions the Holy Family as job-seeking immigrants in *A Regina Construction Site Christmas* (1975).[13] (The image also calls to mind the Ahmanson's sponsorship of the Orange County Rescue Mission, the Village of Hope.) Still, if Kurelek's nativities seem too immediate, a companion piece by Jean Paul Lemieux restores the universality of the scene with a potent dose of satisfying abstraction. The church-like stable is a reminder to Christians that every Eucharistic celebration is Christmas all over again.

But the show-stealing Nativity in this exhibition was made by Alfonso Castillo Orta, with its mariachi wise men, weaving women, and brown baby Christ. Castillo's resplendent nativity evokes the Tree of Jesse images, which—believe it or not—thrived not just at Chartres, but among Puritans as well.[14] Perhaps we can therefore understand the women and men in the branches as not just decoration, but as the descendants of Jesus himself, including Ruth, Tamar, and Uriah (Matthew 1:1-17). This tree is distinctly Meso-American, composed of corn, as if answering the call for a regionally sensitive, environmentally savvy "Green Mariology."[15] The women kneading corn tortillas evoke Christ's ultimate sacrifice, just as European imagery evoked his sacrifice using the subtle symbolism of wheat.[16] More than sentimental folk art, Castillo's *Tree of Life* evokes the sacrifice that ended sacrifice once and for all.[17]

The crowning flower of Castillo's tree is, of course, Our Lady of Guadalupe. The patroness of the Americas has every right to be heavily featured in this Southern California exhibition. But the show surprises us by also including another indigenous, and far less expected, Virgin Mary from Australian Aboriginal culture. Linda Syddick Napaltjarri absorbed both her Aboriginal heritage and Lutheran Christianity thanks to a mission outpost in the central Australian desert. This is how themes such as *Desert Eucharist* or *Wise Men* emerged in her work using the traditional dot painting technique she learned from her uncles. In Syddick's *Nativity*, Mary and Joseph flank the Christ child who envelops them in lassos of love even while an infant. If Mary, for Dante, was *figlia del tuo figlio* (daughter of thy son), then Syddick's image reminds us that Joseph is son of his son as well.

Madonna and Child

For all the beauty of the great ancient icon types such as the *Glykophilousa* (Mary of the Sweet Kiss), there is an irony in the fact that they were painted for the most part by men. How fitting

---

[12] William Kurelek, *A Northern Nativity* (Tundra Books, 1976), 11.

[13] Ibid., 17.

[14] Tara Hamling, *Decorating the 'Godly' Household: Religious Art in Post-Reformation Britain* (Paul Mellon Center, 2011).

[15] Sarah Jane Boss, *Empress and Handmaid: On Nature and Gender in the Cult of the Virgin Mary* (Cassell, 2000); Sarah Jane Boss, *Mary* (New Century Theology), (Continuum, 2004).

[16] For example, Botticelli's 1470 *Madonna of the Eucharist.*

[17] These notions blended seamlessly with pre-Christian Mayan notions of sacrifice. See Jaime Lara, *Christian Texts for Aztecs: Art and Liturgy in Colonial Mexico* (University of Notre Dame Press, 2008).

Opposite: William Kurelek, *Stand in for the Christmas Stable, Alberta,* Detail, 1975

pilgrimages, processions, prayers, and publications all continue.[25] If anything, the Marian tradition, assimilating the best of recent cultural developments, is poised to grow stronger still.

And while all the dimensions of the new (but still ancient) Mary have yet to emerge completely, the Ahmanson collection offers a compelling glimpse of her necessary contours. She is holy but not statically perfect, both green and global, sexual but not sexualized, and acquainted with grief no less than her son. She is immediate and messy, subverting our subversions, but also happy to host a meal. Above all, she did not earn her singular honor of bearing God's Son because she was a well-behaved Jewish girl. As with all of us, it was unmerited grace.

Still, to conclude with that would be too distant, keeping our reflections safe in the realm of thought *about* Mary instead of the entertaining the questions she might direct to us. And this brings us back to that unexpected assortment of individuals that gather for each of the Ahmanson collection events. Mary asks us if—without succumbing to New Age sloppiness or trite psychology—we can bear a truth no less staggering than the Incarnation: That the same God who called her "mother," calls *us*, unmade beds and all, blessed as well.

Matthew J. Milliner
Associate Professor of Art History at Wheaton College

---

[25] The developments (impossible to perfectly track) are nicely gathered in one volume: Sarah Jane Boss, ed. *Mary: The Complete Resource* (Oxford University Press, 2007).

Opposite: Sun Xun, *Pieta*, Detail, 2017

Apostelgeschichte 12. 13.
154
Apostelgeschichte 13, 14.
Das 13. Kapitel.
Das 14. Kapitel.
158
Apostelgeschichte 16. 17.
Das 17. Kapitel.
160
167

Annunciation

Master Paul of Leutschau (Levoča)

Annunciation, circa 1500
Gilt and polychrome on carved linden wood
29 x 28 x 2 inches

Patty Wickman

Overshadowed, 2001
Oil on canvas, 78 x 104 inches

Nativity

Linda Syddick Napaltjarri

Nativity, 2003

Alfonso Castillo Orta

Tree of Life Nativity, 2014
Hand-coiled and painted ceramic,
35 x 26 x 9 inches

Detail Opposite

William Kurelek

Stand in for the Christmas stable, Alberta, 1975
Mixed media on masonite, 24 x 24 inches

William Kurelek

A Regina Construction Site Christmas, 1975
Mixed media on masonite, 24 x 24 inches

Jean Paul Lemieux

Nativité, 1965
Oil on canvas, 27.25 x 16 inches

Madonna and Child

Sir Jacob Epstein

Maquette for Madonna and Child, 1950
Lead and brass wire
13.75 x 5.5 x 5.5 inches

Unknown

Maria Lactans, early 16th century
Oil on panel, arched, 26 x 18.25 inches

Detail Opposite

Dame Barbara Hepworth

Madonna and Child, 1953
Oil and pencil on paper, 19.5 x 15.5 inches

Henry Moore

Madonna and Child, 1943
Terra cotta, 7.5 x 4 x 3 inches

Mary Cassatt

A Kiss for Baby Anne (#1), 1897
Pastel on paper, 25.5 x 20.75 inches

Unknown

Madonna and Child, late 15th century
Tempera on panel with gold ground, 29 x 24 inches

Detail Opposite

Ale Groen

Madonna & Child, 2018
Metal chair frames, steel cable
37.5 x 29.5 x 26 inches

Pietà

Adrian Allinson

Before the Sepulchre, 1944
Oil on canvas, 47.5 x 37.5 inches

Overleaf (detail), and Opposite

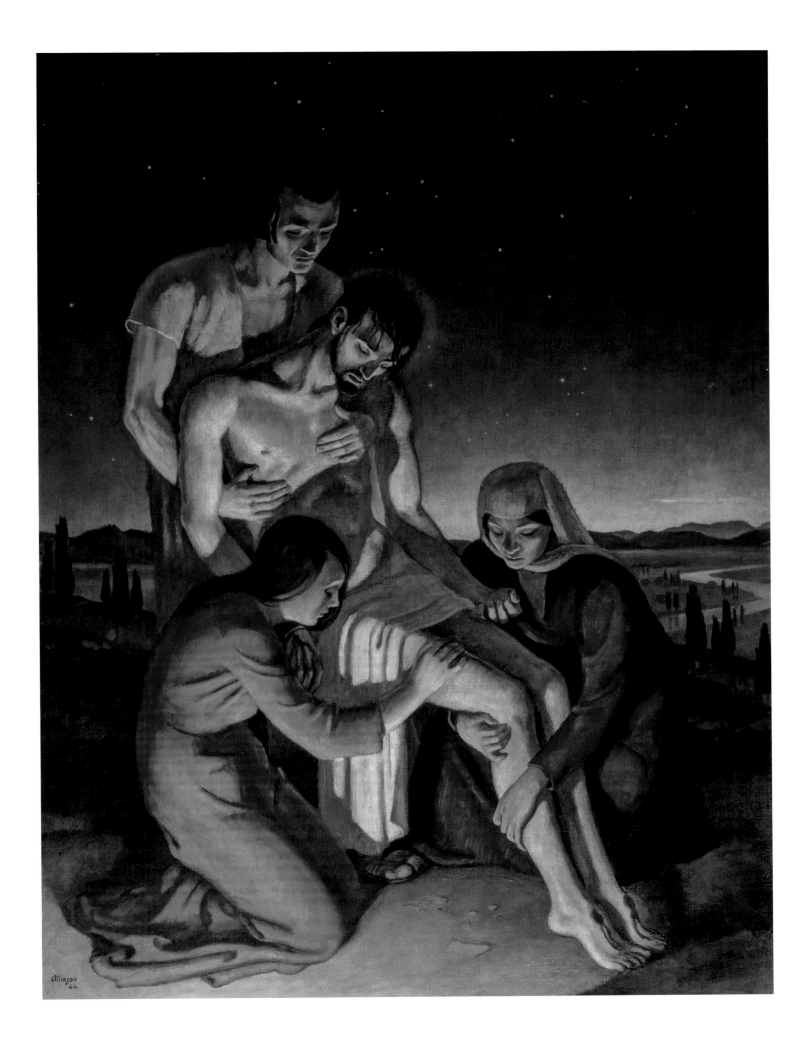

Sun Xun

Pietà, 2017
Paint and ink on original pages from 1896 Martin Luther
translation of the Bible, 53 x 56.3 inches

Georges Rouault

Christ en Croix, 1930
Etching and aquatint in colors on laid Montval paper
Edition 97 of 175, 30.75 x 22.5 inches

Georges Rouault

Christ en Croix (Calvaire), 1930
Oil on paper laid on board, 41 x 29.5 inches

Mary, Mother of God

Nuestra Señora de Guadalupe

Marie Romero Cash

Nuestra Señora de Guadalupe, 2004
Carved wood, 32.5 x 14 x 5 inches

Edward Burra

The Coronation of the Virgin, 1950-52
Watercolor on paper, 80 x 52 inches

Detail Opposite

Patrociño Barela

The Virgin of Guadalupe, 1940
Carved wood, 20.25 x 8.5 x 3.5 inches

Contributors: Roberta Ahmanson, John Silvis, and Matthew J. Milliner
ISBN: 978-1-7324212-3-3
Project Manager: Ann Hirou
Book Design: Reynolds Wulf Inc.
Robert M. Reynolds, Letha Gibbs Wulf
Photography: Eric Stoner
Editor: Deanna Oothoudt
Printed and bound in the United States:
GLS Companies, Saint Paul, Minnesota